12447

BUTTERFIELD SCHOOL
1441 LAKE STREET
LIBERTYVILLE, IL 60048

DEMCO

The Appaloosa

Rachel Damon Criscione

The Rosen Publishing Group's
PowerKids Press™
New York

To Terry Starkweather, thanks for being you.

Published in 2007 by The Rosen Publishing Group, Inc.
29 East 21st Street, New York, NY 10010

First Edition

Editors: Melissa Acevedo and Amelie Von Zumbusch
Book Design: Ginny Chu
Photo Credits: Cover, title page, p.15 © Kit Houghton/Corbis; p. 4 © Prenzel Photo/Animals Animals; p. 7 Appaloosa Museum & Heritage Center; p. 8 © John McAnulty/Corbis; pp. 10, 11 Library of Congress Prints and Photographs Division; p. 12 © Bob Langrish; p. 14 © Robert Maier/Animals Animals; p. 16 © Michael S. Lewis/Corbis; p.19 Courtesy of the Appaloosa Horse Club; p. 20 Photo and pedigree courtesy of Tammy Severson / Bear Creek Appaloosas, Paints and Quarter Horses.

Library of Congress Cataloging-in-Publication Data

Criscione, Rachel Damon.
  The Appaloosa / Rachel Damon Criscione.— 1st ed.
      p. cm. — (The Library of horses)
  Includes bibliographical references and index.
  ISBN 1-4042-3450-0 (lib. bdg.)
  1. Appaloosa horse—Juvenile literature. I. Title.
  SF293.A7C75 2007
  636.1'3—dc22
                                                2005026677

Manufactured in the United States of America

Table of Contents

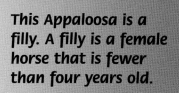

This Appaloosa is a filly. A filly is a female horse that is fewer than four years old.

A One-of-a-Kind Horse

The Appaloosa is a type of horse that is known for its colorful coat patterns. The horse's markings range from just a few dots to an allover spotted pattern. This type of markings makes this horse special because no two Appaloosas have the same pattern.

Spanish colonists brought horses to America during the sixteenth century. At this time Native Americans were already living in America, or the New World. They had never seen horses before. Over time the Native Americans captured some of the Spanish horses. The Native Americans soon grew to prize the horses' grace and beauty. Today's Appaloosas come from some of the horses that Native Americans owned.

Hunting Horses

After some time in the New World, Spanish colonists forced the Native Americans into slavery. In the 1680s, the Native American slaves drove the colonists away for a short time. The slaves kept the cattle that had belonged to the Spanish but traded the horses to other Native American nations. This is how horses ended up north of where the Spanish settled. In the early 1700s, the Nez Percé nation, which lived in present-day Washington, Idaho, and Oregon, began **breeding** the Appaloosa.

The Nez Percé trained the horses to help them hunt. They soon found that the Appaloosas were good at tracking buffalo. The horses were able to keep pace with the buffalo as their riders hung on with their legs. This made the Appaloosa important to the Nez Percé.

This picture was taken around 1922. It shows two women from the Nez Percé nation riding their Appaloosa horses.

The name "Appaloosa" comes from the Palouse River. The Palouse River runs through the state of Washington, which was part of the original Nez Percé country.

A Gift from the Gods

It is not known exactly why the Appaloosa has become commonly tied with the Nez Percé and not other Native American nations. It may be because it is believed that the Nez Percé were the first to start breeding these horses.

In the New World during the sixteenth century, some nations' wealth depended on the number of horses they owned. The Nez Percé differed from these nations because they thought only of their horses' condition. Because they wanted the best horses, the Nez Percé started breeding the strongest and fastest **stallions** with the best **mares**. They did this so the new horses that were born would have the best features of their parents. This is how the Nez Percé began breeding the Appaloosa.

The Nez Percé War

This picture of Chief Joseph was taken in 1900.

The northwestern movement of white settlers in the 1800s changed the fate of the Nez Percé and the Appaloosa forever. By that time some of the New World had become the United States. The U.S. government had decided that white settlers should have the land that had belonged to the Nez Percé. Then the nation would live on a **reservation**. This started the Nez Percé War in 1877.

Chief Joseph, the Nez Percé leader, wanted to keep his people's freedom. The Nez Percé traveled more than 1,300 miles (2,092 km) north to escape the U.S. Army.

This drawing from 1877 shows the Nez Percé War in Montana. This war led to the capture of Chief Joseph.

However, they were caught and forced onto reservations. They were also forced to give up their Appaloosa horses to the U.S. government, which either sold or killed the horses.

Appaloosas have many special features that set them apart from other horses. You can recognize an Appaloosa by its mottled skin and its sclera.

A Horse of Many Colors

Because of their colorful coats and special markings, no two Appaloosas look exactly alike. However, all Appaloosa horses have several features in common. Appaloosas have **mottled** skin under their coats. This means that their skin is pink with dark spots. No other kind of horse has this sort of skin. Appaloosas also have thick black-and-white hooves. They are striped like a zebra's.

One of the most unusual features of an Appaloosa is its eyes. A white ring called a sclera surrounds the iris, or the colored center of the eye. All horses have a sclera, but it is only noticeable when a horse widens its eyes in anger or fear. An Appaloosa's sclera is easier to see than that of any other **breed** of horse. Some people think the Appaloosa's eyes look like human eyes.

Shows and Races

There are several horse shows for Appaloosas. In these shows judges look at the horses and rate their beauty. The judges also rate how well the horses have been trained. The winners are given prizes.

Appaloosas also take part in races that are like the games that the Nez Percé played when learning how to ride horses. One such race is the Nez Percé Stake Race. In this event two horses race each other on separate but **identical** courses. The riders guide their horses through a course of six stakes. The winner then races against other players until there is a final winner.

Appaloosas take part in both Western- and English-style riding events. This horse and its rider are wearing English riding gear.

Appaloosas are gentle creatures that can provide companionship and love for an entire family. This father and his daughter are feeding one of their Appaloosa horses in Moscow, Idaho.

A Well-cared-for Horse

Appaloosa horses need to be well cared for to take part in races and shows. Like all horses Appaloosas need food, housing, water, and exercise. Every day an average full-grown Appaloosa eats about 14 pounds (6 kg) of grass and hay and between 4 and 12 quarts (4 and 11 l) of oats and **bran**. However, if a horse is expected to work a lot, it may be given extra food. Carrots are often given to horses as a gift for good conduct.

Appaloosas can live up to 30 years. People who own Appaloosas keep their horses healthy by taking them to a **veterinarian**. The veterinarian can tell the owner what kind of food and drugs the horse needs. The veterinarian also does any necessary dental work on the horse's teeth.

Recognizing an Appaloosa

Providing an Appaloosa with proper care depends on an owner's knowledge of the horse's **heritage**. Appaloosas can have parents that are quarter horses, Morgans, or Arabians. This varied heritage may also make it hard to recognize a pure Appaloosa.

There are different horse **organizations** that trace a horse's history to prove the horse is from the breed they think it is. There are about eight features that can be used to prove an Appaloosa's heritage. Some of these are the white sclera of the eye, the striped hooves, the facial markings, the mottled skin, and the location of coat patterns. For example, the **blanket pattern** should be over the hips. If the blanket pattern is there, the horse is likely an Appaloosa!

This chart shows the different features used by organizations to recognize a pure Appaloosa horse. The center of the chart shows the sclera, hooves, and mottled skin of an Appaloosa. This chart also shows the different colors and patterns an Appaloosa can have.

Identifying THE APPALOOSA

The Appaloosa has a bold and colorful heritage, originating some 20,000 years ago. Its appearance and unique qualities earned it special recognition in the drawings of cave dwellers, worship in ancient Asia, and status as a prized mount of Spanish explorers, Native Americans and western settlers. Today, the Appaloosa's color, versatility, willing temperament and athletic ability make it a popular choice for a number of activities.

APPALOOSA CHARACTERISTICS

Mottled or Parti-colored Skin

This characteristic is unique to the Appaloosa horse. Therefore, mottled skin is a basic and decisive indicator of an Appaloosa. Mottled skin is different from commonly found pink (flesh-colored or non-pigmented) skin in that it normally contains dark areas of pigmented skin. The result is a speckled or blotchy pattern of pigmented and non-pigmented skin.

White Sclera

The sclera is the area of the eye that encircles the iris — the colored or pigmented portion. The white of the human eye is an example. All horses have sclera and although all horses can show white around the eye if it is rolled back, up or down or if the eyelid is lifted, the Appaloosa's is usually more readily visible than other breeds. All horses can show white around the eye if it is rolled back, up or down or if the eyelid is lifted. Readily visible white sclera is a distinctive Appaloosa characteristic provided it is not in combination with a large white face marking, such as a bald face. An example of sclera is found to the left.

Striped Hooves

Many Appaloosas will have bold and clearly defined vertically light- or dark-striped hooves. An illustration of this characteristic is found to the right.
Vertical stripes may result from an injury to the coronet or a white marking on the leg. Also, light-colored horses tend to have thin stripes in their hooves. As a result, all striped hooves do not necessarily distinguish Appaloosas from non-Appaloosas. Look for other Appaloosa characteristics if any of these situations apply to your horse.

Appaloosas do not always display the above characteristic. In this case, Appaloosa parentage is verified through genetic testing, making these horses eligible for participation in approved Appaloosa Horse Club events. Not all Appaloosa base color, pattern and characteristic combinations are depicted on this chart.

For a free brochure and more information in your area of interest, contact the Appaloosa Horse Club • 2720 W. Pullman Road • Moscow, ID 83843. (208) 882-5578 • (208) 882-8150 FAX • www.appaloosa.com

Illustration by: Sumner Whiteley

Base Color: Blue Roan.
Description: White with spots over entire body.
Face Markings: None.
Leg Markings: None.

Base Color: Dark Bay or Brown.
Description: Roan over body and hips.
Face Markings: Star.
Leg Markings: Lightning marks left fore, partial pastern left hind; lightning marks right fore, partial pastern right hind.

Base Color: Dark Bay or Brown.
Description: Solid.
Face Markings: Star.
Leg Markings: Half-stocking left hind, pastern right hind.

Base Color: Black.
Description: White with spots over loin and hips. Both eyes blue.
Face Markings: Bald face, strip lower lip.
Leg Markings: Stocking left hind, stocking right hind.

Base Color: Bay.
Description: White with spots over loin and hips.
Face Markings: Star, snip, strip lower lip.
Leg Markings: Lightning marks left fore, half-stocking left hind, lightning marks right fore, half-pastern right hind.

Base Color: Buckskin.
Description: Roan over loin and hips.
Face Markings: Star and strip.
Leg Markings: Half-pastern left hind, pastern right hind.

Base Color: Chestnut or Sorrel.
Description: White with spots over back and hips.
Face Markings: Star, stripe and snip.
Leg Markings: Stocking left hind, stocking right fore, partial half-stocking right hind.

Base Color: Dun.
Description: White over back and hips.
Face Markings: None.
Leg Markings: None.

Base Color: Blue Roan.
Description: White with spots over body and hips.
Face Markings: None.
Leg Markings: Partial stocking left hind.

Base Color: Bay Roan.
Description: Spots over body and hips.
Face Markings: None.
Leg Markings: Pastern right fore, ankle right hind.

Base Color: Grulla.
Description: White with spots over back and hips.
Face Markings: Star, stripe and snip.
Leg Markings: Pastern left fore, ankle left hind, half-pastern right fore, half-stocking right hind.

Base Color: Gray.
Description: Solid.
Face Markings: Strip.
Leg Markings: None.

Base Color: Red Roan.
Description: White with spots over back and hips.
Face Markings: Star and snip.
Leg Markings: Pastern left hind, partial half-pastern right fore, lightning marks right hind.

Base Color: Palomino.
Description: White with spots over loin and hips.
Face Markings: Blaze.
Leg Markings: Stockings all four.

19

BRIGHT WINDSTAR *Pedigree*

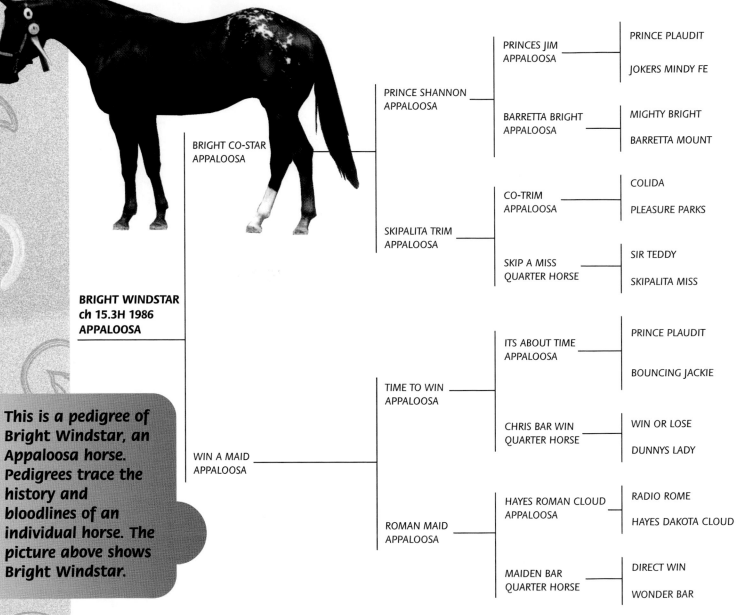

BRIGHT WINDSTAR
ch 15.3H 1986
APPALOOSA

- BRIGHT CO-STAR
  APPALOOSA
  - PRINCE SHANNON
    APPALOOSA
    - PRINCES JIM
      APPALOOSA
      - PRINCE PLAUDIT
      - JOKERS MINDY FE
    - BARRETTA BRIGHT
      APPALOOSA
      - MIGHTY BRIGHT
      - BARRETTA MOUNT
  - SKIPALITA TRIM
    APPALOOSA
    - CO-TRIM
      APPALOOSA
      - COLIDA
      - PLEASURE PARKS
    - SKIP A MISS
      QUARTER HORSE
      - SIR TEDDY
      - SKIPALITA MISS
- WIN A MAID
  APPALOOSA
  - TIME TO WIN
    APPALOOSA
    - ITS ABOUT TIME
      APPALOOSA
      - PRINCE PLAUDIT
      - BOUNCING JACKIE
    - CHRIS BAR WIN
      QUARTER HORSE
      - WIN OR LOSE
      - DUNNYS LADY
  - ROMAN MAID
    APPALOOSA
    - HAYES ROMAN CLOUD
      APPALOOSA
      - RADIO ROME
      - HAYES DAKOTA CLOUD
    - MAIDEN BAR
      QUARTER HORSE
      - DIRECT WIN
      - WONDER BAR

This is a pedigree of Bright Windstar, an Appaloosa horse. Pedigrees trace the history and bloodlines of an individual horse. The picture above shows Bright Windstar.

The Appaloosa Horse Club

There was a time when the Appaloosa almost completely died out. This happened after the Nez Percé War when the U.S. government killed many of these horses.

In 1937, a farmer from Oregon named Claude Thompson read an article about the sad fate of the Nez Percé and their horses. He formed a group to save these horses before it was too late. The group became the Appaloosa Horse Club. This organization traces a horse's heritage using a list of features that Thompson said a horse must have to be a pure Appaloosa. People started to use this list as a guide when breeding horses to create Appaloosas. Soon there were more pure Appaloosas. Today there are more than half a million horses recorded in the Appaloosa Horse Club.

The Chief Joseph Trail Ride

There are many events in which Appaloosas and their riders can take part. One such event is the Chief Joseph Trail Ride. This ride honors the 1,300-mile (2,092 km) journey the Nez Percé and their Appaloosas made in 1877 while trying to escape from the U.S. Army. Each year a group of more than 300 Appaloosas and their owners rides 100 miles (161 km) over several days. They complete the journey over 13 years and start again at the beginning the following year.

When the U.S. Army caught up with the Nez Percé in 1877, they took away most of the Appaloosas and killed or sold them. The breed nearly died out in the early 1900s. However, Appaloosas lived on and became one of the most popular American horse breeds. They are prized throughout the world for their beauty, strength, and history.

Glossary

blanket pattern (BLAN-ket PA-tern) An area of white over the hip or bottom of an Appaloosa horse.

bran (BRAN) A grain made from wheat that is fed to horses.

breed (BREED) A group of animals that look alike and have the same relatives.

breeding (BREED-ing) Bringing a male and a female animal together so they will have babies.

heritage (HER-uh-tij) Parents and other relatives.

identical (eye-DEN-tih-kul) Exactly the same.

mares (MERZ) Adult female horses.

mottled (MAH-tld) Having a pattern of colored spots.

organizations (or-guh-nuh-ZAY-shunz) Groups or societies.

reservation (reh-zer-VAY-shun) An area of land set aside by the government for Native Americans to live on.

stallions (STAL-yunz) Adult male horses.

veterinarian (veh-tuh-ruh-NER-ee-un) A doctor who treats animals.

Index

Web Sites

Due to the changing nature of Internet links, PowerKids Press has developed an online list of Web sites related to the subject of this book. This site is updated regularly. Please use this link to access the list:

www.powerkidslinks.com/horse/appaloos/